There is always more than meets the eye when
it comes to creatures of all kinds. . . .

KATE GARDNER HEIDI SMITH

Lovely BEASTS

The Surprising Truth

BALZER + BRAY
An Imprint of HarperCollinsPublishers

For ZoZo, Josie, and Olive—
the loveliest beasts of all
—K. G.

To my mother and father,
and to God for creating the beautiful animals
which inspired me for this book
—H. S.

Fierce . . .

papa.

As the world's largest primate, gorillas can be surprisingly gentle. They build soft nests for their babies to sleep in at night, groom one another as a way to maintain relationships, and like taking naps.

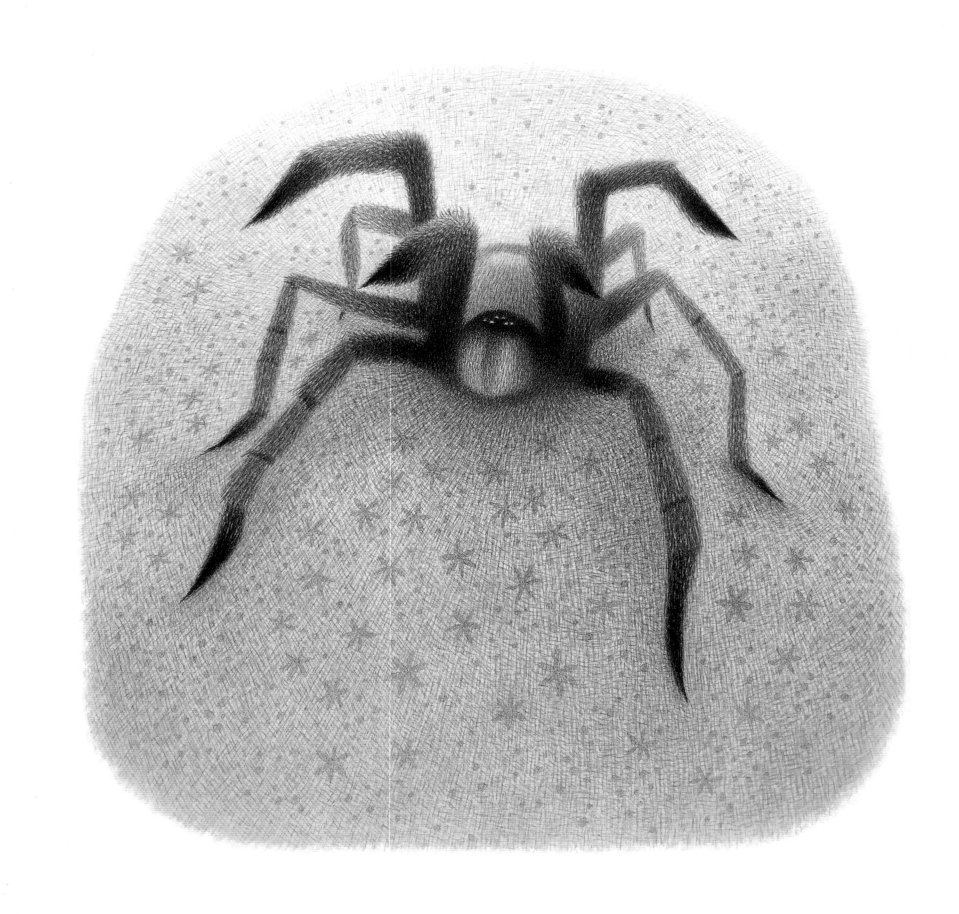

Creepy . . .

crafter.

There are more than 40,000 known species of spiders, and all are amazing creatures with many superhero-like qualities, including the ability to spin intricate webs. While a spider's web can look as fragile and delicate as a snowflake, it's incredibly strong. For its weight, spider silk is stronger than steel!

Tough . . .

but vulnerable.

Rhinoceroses might look like nothing can hurt them, but their populations hover close to extinction due to human hunters and loss of land to building and development. Sadly, there are no known northern white rhinos left in the wild at all, and the ones in captivity (in Kenya) number just two: Fatu and Najin.

Fanged . . .

friend.

Stories such as "Little Red Riding Hood" and "The Three Little Pigs" present wolves as big, bad, and scary. The reality is that wolves are highly social animals who live, play, and hunt in tight-knit packs or families of up to fifteen members. While their nighttime howls may send shivers down your spine, it's just their way of talking with one another and saying, *Hey, I'm over here!*

Prickly . . .

but gentle.

When threatened by a predator, porcupines can raise their needle-sharp quills as a reminder that they are not a good or easy meal (it's a myth that they can shoot their quills, though they dislodge easily if someone gets too close). Left alone, they are shy herbivores who eat leaves, flower blossoms, and berries.

Buzzing . . .

busy workers.

Bees don't want to sting you—in fact, honeybees die after they use their stingers. They'd rather focus on what they do best: making delicious honey. If they do sting you, it's likely because they want to keep you away from their hive and hard work. After all, bees have to visit more than two million flowers to make just one pound of honey!

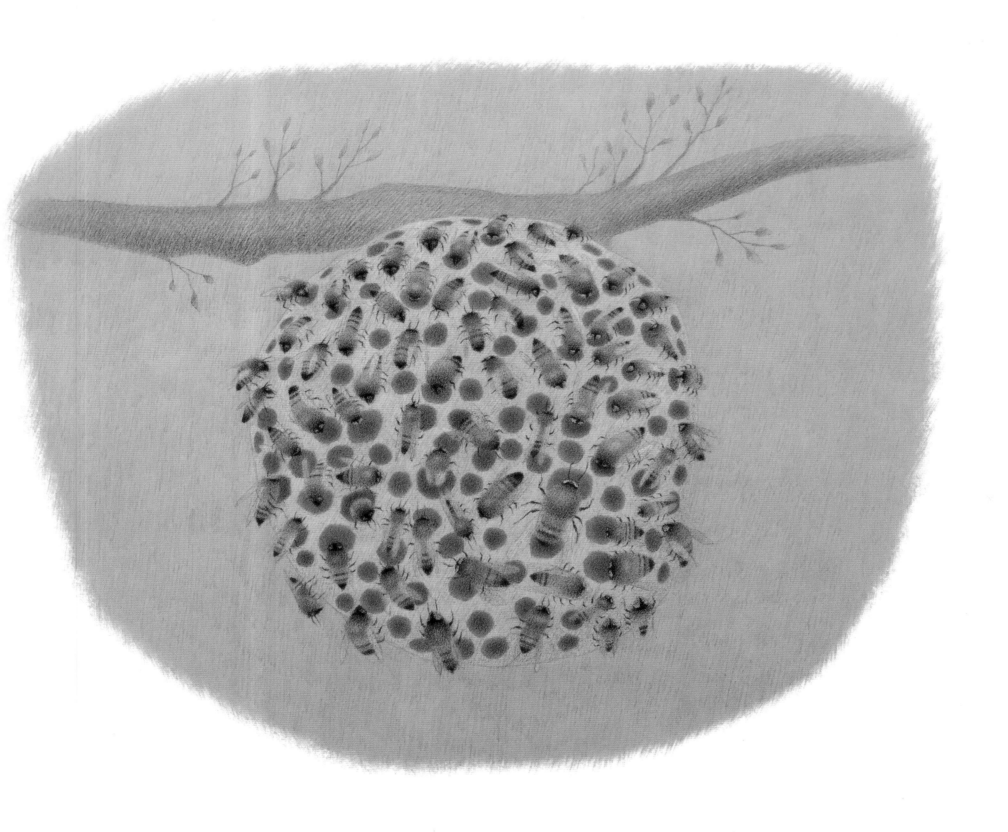

Slimy . . .

genius.

With eight suckered arms, a beak, blue blood, and three hearts, octopuses might seem like aliens. But they are also playful, intelligent, and strong. One of their many tricks is to camouflage themselves in their environment—both with color and texture—as a way to hide in plain sight from predators. Can you spot the octopus?

Ugly . . .

caretaker.

With over a thousand species, some bats might be considered cuter than others. Regardless of looks, many bats play an important role in the environment by controlling insect populations, eating as many as eight thousand mosquitoes a night. Flying fox bats help to replant forests—certain seeds won't sprout until they're first eaten, digested, and excreted by bats—while fruit-eating bats disperse pollen when it clings to their fur during nighttime foraging. Much of the tropical rainforest wouldn't exist without bats' help!

Sharp-toothed . . .

guardian.

Sharks—especially great white sharks—are almost universally feared. But sharks are not the man-eaters movies and stories have made them out to be. Your chances of being killed by a shark are one in thirty-seven million, while the reverse odds are not in sharks' favor: each year, humans kill one hundred million sharks worldwide. Sharks are at the top of the food chain and help maintain the health and biodiversity of our oceans. Without them, the entire marine ecosystem would collapse.

Big . . .

bigger . . .

biggest . . .

leaders.

With their great size, speed, and strength, these proud mamas are rare examples of matriarchy in the animal kingdom. That means that female hyenas, lionesses, and elephants are the head of their families. Female hyenas are 10 percent bigger than males and are at the top of the social ladder of their clans, while lionesses do all the hunting and provide meals for their pride. Elephant herds are led by the oldest and biggest female, who carefully watches over everyone and leads the way.

Giant or small,
wondrous and strange

. . . beautiful, *lovely* beasts.

To Learn More:

Alexander, Kwame. *Animal Ark: Celebrating Our Wild World in Poetry and Pictures*. Washington, DC: National Geographic, 2017.

Grundmann, Emmanuelle. *Zoo-ology*. Illustrated by Joëlle Jolivet. New York: Roaring Brook, 2003.

Hegarty, Patricia. *Above and Below*. Illustrated by Hanako Clulow. Tulsa: Kane Miller, 2017.

Jenkins, Steve. *Actual Size*. Boston: Houghton Mifflin Harcourt, 2004.

Messner, Kate. *Over and Under the Snow*. Illustrated by Christopher Silas Neal. San Francisco: Chronicle, 2011.

Sidman, Joyce. *Dark Emperor & Other Poems of the Night*. Illustrated by Rick Allen. Boston: Houghton Mifflin Harcourt, 2010.

Williams, Lily. *If Sharks Disappeared*. New York: Roaring Brook, 2017.

For Older Readers:

Broom, Jenny. *Animalium: Welcome to the Museum*. Somerville: Big Picture, 2014.

Montgomery, Sy. *The Great White Shark Scientist*. Boston: Houghton Mifflin Harcourt, 2016.

Sartore, Joel. *The Photo Ark: One Man's Quest to Document the World's Animals*. Washington, DC: National Geographic, 2017.